I0163730

THE

ROADMAP

TO

STRESS

BY GEORGE BISSETT

DEDICATION

This book is dedicated to my three daughters – Dorothy, Terri, and Lynette – and their families. Just because.

ACKNOWLEDGEMENTS

Bob Bray is my friend and business partner; Bob and his wife, Dawn, motivated me to write out what I had so many times talked to them about. If you check out our website (www.dynamicdiscovery.ca) you will see that Bob has excellent 'helping" skills of his own.

I have gained much fun and insight from my Saturday morning "breakfast club" members; Gord, Mannie, Mike, Bob, and Cliff. These guys are both hilarious and wise at the same time. Thanks for the stories and support. And I apologize for all the times I skipped out when it was my turn to pay – but there will be no reimbursement.

And heartfelt thanks to Christina (Chrissy) Rice who has organized and formatted my words and has been the driving force behind getting this book published.

TABLE OF CONTENTS

WHY WE REFERENCE HRS

In Our Workshop Information
Throughout this piece you will find references to HRS so I will provide a bit of background: HRS is an Employee Assistance Program provider who works with more than 100 professionals to provide counseling assistance to troubled persons to help them solve their problems – whether home or work-related.

HRS is called upon for many and varied reasons, but a common reason is because the family of today generally faces a more difficult and / or stressful life than our parents and grandparents experienced. In part it has to do with lifestyle shifts which often create economic burdens that are more intense now than ever, and which is why one of the major concerns of employees is work or job security. Today, we have to work 80 hours to produce the same economic benefit our parents produced in 45 hours, and most of us receive only 80% of our sleep requirement. Of course this impacts the worker, but it also has a great effect on the family through the decrease of what is popularly referred to as "Quality Time".

Over the years, HRS developed several workshops and Seminars, all of which were structured from reality experience as opposed to theoretical premises. They are not guesses – they are an application of the outcomes from the results experienced from working with some 50,000 clients.

Since 50,000 case files provide for a significant database, the various programs are result oriented and have predictable outcomes. This experience has proven invaluable in a real understanding of human behaviors which has proven to be extremely useful in the development of programs for changing or modifying human behavior, which in turn provides a strong base to all of the other workshop /seminar topics that HRS developed. Although I brought my own workshop and seminar programs with me when I joined HRS more than 20 years ago, I also learned from so many others who worked with HRS over many years. Dynamic Discovery is now offering many workshops/seminars that cover all problematic situations that humans encounter merely from living, breathing and working.

WHAT IS STRESS?

A simple definition is that stress is the "wear and tear" our bodies experience as we adjust to our continually changing environment; it has physical and emotional effects on us and can create poor or negative feelings. Stress will help or hinder us, depending on how we react to it.

As a positive influence, stress can help compel us to action; it can result in a new awareness and an exciting new perspective.

As a negative influence, it can result in feelings of distrust, rejection, anger, and depression, which in turn can lead to health problems such as headaches, upset stomach, rashes, insomnia, ulcers, high blood pressure, heart disease, and stroke. With the death of a loved one, birth of a child, job promotion, or a new intimate relationship, we experience stress as we readjust our lives. When adjusting to different circumstances, stress will help or hinder us depending on how we react to it.

How Can I Eliminate Stress From My Life?

So-called positive stress (eustress) adds anticipation and excitement to life, and we all are under a certain amount of stress. Deadlines, competitions, confrontations, and even frustrations and sorrows add depth and enrichment to our lives. Our goal is not to eliminate stress but to learn how to manage it and how to use it to help us. Insufficient stress acts as a depressant and may leave us feeling bored or dejected; on the other hand, excessive stress may leave us feeling "tied up in knots." What we need to do is find the optimal level of stress to individually motivate, but not overwhelm, each of us.

How Can I Tell What The Optimal Stress For Me Is?

There is no single level of stress that is optimal for all people. We are all individual creatures with unique requirements. As such, what is distressing to one may be a joke to another. And even when we agree that a particular event is distressing, we are likely to differ in our physiological response to it. For instance, the person who loves to arbitrate disputes, moving from job site to job site, would be stressed in a stable and routine job, whereas the person who thrives under stable conditions would very likely be stressed on a job where duties were highly varied and mobile.

Another Plague?

Throughout history, mankind has had periodic episodes of illness which have decimated the population. The Bubonic Plague ravaged Europe in the Middle Ages. Syphilis killed one in four Europeans when it was introduced to Europe in the 1500's. Every other Hawaiian was killed by measles in the 1700's. Meanwhile, North American Indians were slain by smallpox and other imported diseases.

Today, it is reported that one in ten North Americans are falling victim to OVERSTRESS. Those who are becoming chemically dependent are walking a fatal path. Others "drop out" at an early age, joining the ranks of society's "marginal survivors".

TO YOUR BODY, STRESS IS SYNONYMOUS WITH
CHANGE. Anything that causes a change in your life
causes stress. It doesn't matter if it is "good" change, or
"bad" change, they are both stress. When you find your
dream house and get ready to move, that is stress. If you
break your leg, that is stress. Good or bad, if it is a
CHANGE in your life, it is stress as far as your body is
concerned.

The Stress Cycle
(Read Clockwise From The Top)

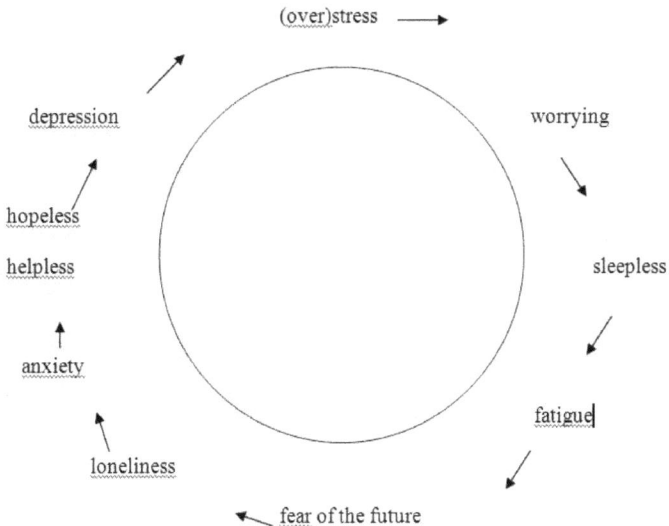

(over)stress ⟶

depression · worrying · hopeless · helpless · sleepless · anxiety · fatigue · loneliness · fear of the future

Even IMAGINED CHANGE is stressful. (We call it
"worrying".) If you fear that you will not have enough
money to pay your mortgage or rent that is stress. If you

worry that you may get fired, that is stress. If you think that you may receive a promotion at work that is also stress (even though this would be a good change). Whether the event is good or bad, imagining changes in your life is stressful.

Anything that causes CHANGE IN YOUR DAILY ROUTINE is stressful. Anything that causes CHANGE IN YOUR BODY HEALTH is stressful. IMAGINED CHANGES are just as stressful as real changes.

The cost of OVERSTRESS to North American society is immense. Some reports suggest the cost to be $300 Billion per year, at least! Our society loses through lost productivity, medical care, job accidents, and traffic fatalities.

Valley Chart

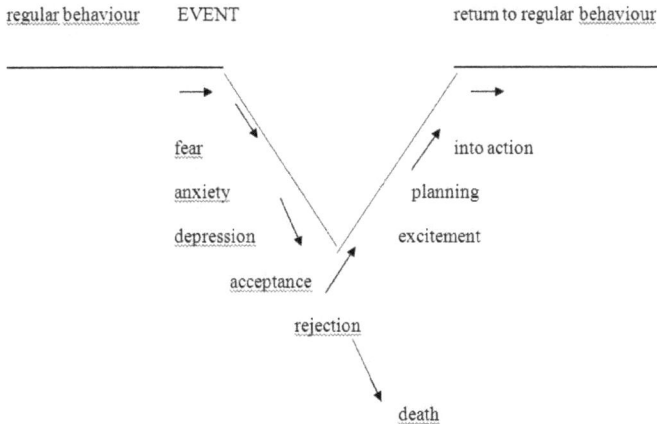

Certainly, we live in a society whose hallmark is rapid change. Our broader definition of stress tells us that this rapid change means high stress levels. Most of the human experience has not prepared us to handle the demands of life today. And that is why HRS placed such a value on stress management programs since once the clients' overstress was dealt with they could then help them to deal with their other problems.

As EFAP providers, HRS worked with people to help them find a solution to their problems – all of which are stress-related or provoked by stress. Generalized information taken from a random review of HRS case files shows that, upon assessment, the average number of problems per client was 4.75, and more than 60% of the problems dealt with fell into 5 general categories, as follows:

1. Stress / distress 15.04 % (*)
2. Family (includes adolescence & blended family) 17.60 %
3. Communication 12.82 %
4. Health (includes physical, mental, eating disorders, psychological, psychiatric, mental abuse, and physical abuse)   10.15 %
5. Alcohol / drug 9.56 %

(*) the stress / distress category refers when it is necessary for a client to get their level of stress in control prior to being able to deal with the major problem being experienced.

EUSTRESS VS. DISTRESS

Many people are unaware that there are two categories of stress: Eustress and Distress.

Eustress is the good stress that motivates you to continue working. Stress can be a motivator and provide incentive to get the job done. This "good stress" is what eustress can be identified as and some people enjoy it. Everyone needs a little bit of stress in their life in order to continue to be happy, motivated, challenged and productive. It is when this stress is no longer tolerable and/or manageable that distress comes in.

Bad stress, or distress, is when the good stress becomes too much to bear or cope with. Tension builds, there is no longer any fun in the challenge, there seems to be no relief, no end in sight. This is the kind of stress most of us are familiar with and this is the kind of stress that leads to poor decision making. Physiological symptoms of distress include an increase in blood pressure, rapid breathing and generalized tension. Behavioral symptoms include overeating, loss of appetite, drinking, smoking and negative coping mechanisms.

Stress tolerance is the power to endure stress. If you feel stress, whether you lose to it or not all depends on your stress tolerance. A person's tolerance to stress is not only different according to the person but is also influenced by time and condition. So tolerance to stress may differ largely to the same person according to the time and condition in which it is experienced. Mainly, the personality and physique, environment and condition change the strength of tolerance to stress.

The trick to coping with stress is not to expect that you can eliminate it but, rather, to manage the symptoms of stress. Teaching you how to do that has become a multi-million dollar industry. But in the end, it all boils down to a few good tried-and-true skills you can learn and the willingness to work at it.

Ways to Become Stress-Resistant

- Stop feeling guilty.
- Be decisive.
- Avoid being a perfectionist.
- Set priorities for yourself.
- Stop procrastinating.
- Praise yourself.
- Live an optimal lifestyle.

DEVELOPING EUSTRESS

Without eustress we are not equipped to deal with excitement and/or challenge in our lives. It is eustress that fuels our successes and achievements. You may be experiencing eustress if you feel eager, excited, thrilled, proud, resilient, determined, fulfilled or in a state of flow.

Eustress is defined as moderate or normal psychological stress interpreted as being beneficial for the one experiencing it.

1). Distressing and tough circumstances can also lead us to experience healthy eustress – as we learn to cope and develop greater strength, determination and courage.
In the short term eustress provides us with an energy boost to perform challenging activities – especially where we need to focus and put in extra effort e.g. playing

competitive sport or public speaking/delivering a seminar.

2) In the longer term, eustress helps us keep working at things – especially when the going gets tough e.g. learning and growing as get on with our lives after a rejection or keeping on studying when we'd really rather give up!

In short, stress can be good! Eustress helps us achieve things of meaning and value to us, leading us to feel better about ourselves – and grow in confidence and stature.

Here Are 9 Examples of Eustress

1). GETTING TO KNOW SOMEONE we really like – a new friend, colleague or romantic interest.

2). STUDYING for a new qualification over a period of time - sustaining us as we work towards something bigger that will move us forwards in life like a new qualification.

3). LEARNING and ADAPTING to new routines and cultures when TRAVELLING. When we travel, we must get out of our routines and comfort zones – and adapt to different foods, time zones, customs, language/s, scenery and more.

4). NETWORKING and CONNECTING with others to grow ourselves and our businesses. Meeting lots of new people at once and showing ourselves and what we do to a larger world.

5). PERFORMING at our best when we play COMPETITIVE SPORTS or a fitness activity. Eustress helps us perform better in the moment AND also to improve ourselves by staying committed to our exercise routine even when we may not feel like it.

6). PREPARING for and working towards BIG GOALS or EVENTS like getting married, having a baby, getting a new job or promotion.

7). DEVELOPING NEW SKILLS especially where we have to practice to improve and work through the awkward beginner's stage e.g. learning a new hobby, language or sport.

8). GETTING OVER A REJECTION – whether it's a job, relationship or some other opportunity, eustress sustains us and helps us learn, grow as individuals – and find the silver lining.

9). STAYING THE COURSE with personal development - even when it gets tough. This is especially relevant for coaching and therapy. It's eustress that will help our clients keep working on themselves and turning up for coaching sessions even when the going gets tough…

So, any time we are out of our comfort zones, but working towards something bigger or feel excited or challenged in a good way, eustress is at work. Without eustress our lives would be pretty dull – and hard work!

It really is all in the mind. Whether something is considered eustress or distress depends on:
1.   Our reaction to the stimulus AND
2.   How in control of a situation we feel.

For example networking could be considered eustress for some people (who consider it fun or a challenge) and for others it may feel DIStressing. Or we may feel eustress if we asked for a promotion and start a new, more challenging role. But we may feel DIStress if we are told we MUST perform a role which we don't feel equipped to do well.

Final thought: Think about how you can reframe your DIStress into more positive and helpful Eustress.

"When we accept tough jobs as a challenge to our ability and wade into them with joy and enthusiasm, miracles can happen." - Arland Gilbert

Stress Summary

The number of people who report "feeling highly stressed" has more than doubled over the past decade. Changing organizational and societal structures, increasing demands on our time, and constant reminders to build the perfect career, marriage, and life have all escalated to a frenzied where's-the-panic-button epidemic. But before you push it, remember that some stress is good.

Stress is simply the body's non-specific response to any demand made on it. By definition, then, it does not come packed with tension and anxiety, or exhaustion and illness. As the body responds to various forms of stress, whether good or bad, certain changes occur. The increased heart rate and secretions of hormones that stimulate your body are typical of this "fight or flight" response. You need and activate this response in order to accomplish all sorts of tasks, from meeting a deadline to completing those agonizing last minutes of a grueling run. Stress does increase your productivity, but has its limits.

Too much stress, or an intense period of negative events, can wear down your body's ability to cope with stress. Over time, it can lead to chronic pain, anxiety, fatigue, addiction, and headaches. Moreover, stress has been linked to heart disease, cancer, lung ailments, accidents, cirrhosis, and suicide. In fact, the US Centre for Disease Control reports than more than half of the deaths under the age of 65 result from stressful lifestyles.

The challenge, then, lies in optimizing the amount of stress we need in our lives. It is also crucial to be able to recognize and deal with those times when we feel tense, overworked or burdened.

We all get into ruts where frustrations and anxiety build up as a result of changes or unpleasant events. That is inevitable. It will happen to you. But before throwing in the towel and burying your head in the sand like a ruffled ostrich, know that there's a plus side. What isn't inevitable is how can control the way you cope with such turns in your life. You are capable of seizing your life's steering wheel, u-turning it, and heading towards a focused and satisfying path to well-being.

Start small and reap the rejuvenating rewards. Instead of finding solace with the jujubes and the boob tube, discover some outlets. No not shopping ones, although to many it can be a comfort. We're talking physical outlets, and not just the sweat-til- you've-replenished-the-Sahara-types of activities. Great ones include tai chi, yoga, and weight training in addition to more demanding sports such as running, tennis, and basketball. The key is finding those that are to your liking, and fit your schedule and lifestyle. There's really no point in signing up for an early riser aquafit class if your concept of a head start on the day is getting up early enough to beat the breakfast menu changeover at McDonald's.

Regardless of the activity you choose, upping the physical fitness ante makes you less vulnerable to stress responses. The heart and circulation are able to work harder for longer stretches. The muscles, ligaments, bones, and joints become stronger and more flexible. And the mind is often better able to cope with stress and stay on an even, happier keel. What's more, you're more likely to feel energized and better about your appearance. It's also a great way to meet other people, and bond with those you already know.

Physical fitness is just one of many ways to exercise your stress demons. Try a few, try many. Not all methods work for all people. For instance, many people try running but get bored of the monotony. Others end up joining a gym and involve themselves in a variety of up-tempo step and kick-box classes. Along with a healthy diet and setting realistic goals, we have the ability to drive ourselves out of the deep downtrodden ditch of stress. Adopt some coping strategies of your own and stressful times can be more hype than horror.

PLAN TO AVOID STRESS

A little planning can go a long way in reducing stress, which is largely self-imposed by poor time management habits.

Take finances, for example. Work out your portfolio of assets, forecast your long-term financial needs, and estimate what you should be putting aside on a regular basis. Stress can be significantly reduced by following simple advice such as not giving in to impulses, and buying only what you really need. Impulses may be satisfying for the short-term, but lead to headaches in the long run.

Some habits are stressful in and of themselves. If you are a chronic "Yes"-er, get in the habit of saying "No", especially when you know deep down inside that you are taking on more than you can handle.

Or even thinking of situations as stressful can be doubly stressful! If, for example, you are conditioned to freak out about the morning commute, worrying about the possibility of an accident or getting stuck in a traffic jam, you are going to be stressed out about the drive, even if you give yourself plenty of time to get to your destination.

So how can you avoid these stress-inducing habits? Plan! Organize your life. Know what your true obligations are. Say "no" to the tasks and situations which are avoidable and which won't turn your life upside down if you don't attend to them.

Prioritize the most important tasks. Make a game plan of what you seek to accomplish for the day. Check them off as you complete them. Reward yourself for meeting your goals.

If you can, delegate your tasks. Do you have to be the one to fix the toilet, scrub the floor, pick up the kids from school, and buy the groceries?

Think about situations where stress can be avoided. For example, if girlfriend calls saying she will be an hour late, is that a reason to get stressed out? If your waiter forgets to bring you that glass of water you requested, should you go bonkers? Little things can add up, so avoid piling on to the point of reaching stress overload. After all, will it matter five months down the road? How about five minutes even?

Of course, some stress is good, as it spurs commitment, determination, and desire. But taking tiny steps to avoid the equally tiny bumps can go a long way to smoothing out your life path.

IDENTIFYING STRESSORS AND LISTENING TO YOUR BODY

Body Stressors are those things that elicit stress in you.
Learning to identify these is the first step to overcoming
the harmful effects of stress and taking control of your
life. Anything that makes you angry, sad, frightened,
surprised, excited or happy can cause you stress. When
you are stressed your body undergoes a number of
changes. The symptoms of stress, like stressors, are
varied and depend on the individual-here are some
common ones:

Physical Symptoms:

- High blood pressure
- Headaches
- Chest pain
- Fatigue

- Eyestrain
- Back pain
- Constipation or Diarrhea
- Shortness of breath
- Stiff neck
- Upset stomach
- Weight gain/loss

Emotional Signs

- Depression
- Irritability
- Low self-esteem
- Anger
- Apathy
- Anxiety

Behavioral Indicators

- Over or under eating
- Increased smoking
- Increased drinking
- Forgetfulness

- Insomnia
- Careless driving
- Problems with relationships.

•Identifying your symptoms and connecting them with stressors gives you a starting point from where you can begin to manage your stress.

THE MENTAL AND PHYSIOLOGICAL EFFECTS OF STRESS

The Stress Response can be Good and Bad for you.

The stress response is your body's reaction to a situation you find stressful.

Surprisingly, the body reacts similarly to good and bad events. Stress responses are necessary for us to cope with situations that excite or disturb us; they can be very useful.

Stage 1

Your body's first response is to release adrenaline. This hormone increases your heart and breathing rates and gives you a jolt of energy to take on an immediate challenge.

Your mind will also become preoccupied with the stressful situation in this first stage.

This stage is great if your problem requires immediate action. In fact, many people do their best work under pressure. If your problem can't be dealt with right away and your burst of adrenaline doesn't help you identify a solution, this response is just exciting you for nothing.

Stage 2

Assuming your situation persists, your body will begin to consume stored energy resources. At this point you will likely feel driven, pressured, preoccupied, and possibly tired. Often, this is when individuals engage in maladaptive coping responses; increased drinking, smoking, and unhealthy eating are common, as is anti-social behavior and reduced exercise. This is odd as all of these things actually reduce peoples' social and biological abilities to cope with stress.

Stage 3

At this point in the stress cycle the mere thought of the stressful situation elicits anxiety, feelings of helplessness and/or hopelessness. Irritability, anger, memory loss and depressed immune functioning may make you more susceptible to illnesses at this point.

Stage 4

After a long period of continuous stress, your body's need for energy outstrips available resources, and chronic stress results; this is bad. Insomnia, errors in judgment, excessive anxiety, depression, panic attacks, and personality changes often occur at this point. As well, serious illness may result as a consequence of depressed immune system functioning and prolonged excitatory responses. This is your body's way of forcing you to relax, even if it means that you do so in the hospital.

STRESS, ANXIETY AND ANGER

Stress

Modern living has become synonymous with stressful living. No longer do humans aimlessly roam the countryside, killing and eating the odd woolly mammoth. Today, if fluctuations in the stock market don't stress you out, there's always the mortgage and that phone call from your kid's school to worry about.

Fight the Grinch!

The season of snowflakes and mistletoe is upon us but many of us don't share St. Nick's jolly sentiments when it comes to the holidays. This winter, psychological strain, as well as financial and time crunches, highlight the reasons for our discontent. Modern life makes stress a fact of life. Learn to cope as you share your thoughts and experiences.

According to a recent survey by a leading opinion research firm, gift shopping, time constraints, and elevated expenses topped the list of holiday woes for workers in North America. But there are other culprits for the holiday blues as well. For many, spending the holidays alone for the first time can easily become depressed during the holidays. Similarly, watching holiday joy blossom in others can make it especially difficult for those already suffering from loneliness, depression, or feelings of isolation. If you are in this kind of situation don't hold your emotions back but instead acknowledge them because they are normal and understandable. The sooner you let them out the sooner you'll be able to clear your head, seek out solutions, and move on with your life.

In addition to personal turmoil, the holidays are primetime for family conflicts. One of the main reasons for this is that often it's the only time of year where the entire family makes a concerted effort to come together. And sometimes, despite the best intentions, the reasons for such sparse encounters between family members become painfully obvious during these annual reunions.

Differences between extended family members are not as common as those involving immediate family. For instance the simple question of where to spend the holidays can be a sore point for many families. Mom thinks the family should travel west to see grandma and grandpa. But dad's parents are holidaying in the sunny South, and after a couple months bitter Northern cold where the family lives, the decision is a virtual no-brainer for dad. Dad's assumptions combined with mom's strong feelings for her parents makes for a situation with the explosive power of Uncle Albert's gut, and the destructive power of Aunt Alice's 'legendary' fruitcake dropped from 20,000 ft!

High expectations for the holidays are normal but are your expectations reasonable? Do you expect that Uncle Albert's belt-loosening at the table will be any less irritating? Or will your sister's ill-mannered children grabbing food off of your plate offend you any less this year? Things go wrong during the holidays; so before you tell Uncle Albert to solve the energy crisis with his fat stores, recognize that Martha Stewart memories exist only in dreams and glossy paged magazines. Another way to make things go as smooth as possible during the holidays is to set aside differences with other family members. If politics get everyone all hot and bothered just don't talk about them … set ground rules if you have to.

Part of being realistic during the holidays is being ready to accept that not everyone you want to hook up with will be able to. This is not your fault so don't take it personally! The holidays are a busy time of family obligations, overtime hours, mad shopping, and more.

Be flexible and understanding when it comes to meeting with friends and family… but don't bend yourself out of shape. Recognize that you have limitations like everyone else.

Keeping the Grinch at bay can also involve getting help when you need it. If you haven't any family or dependable friends nearby, why not take advantage of whatever social support is available to you? Visit your local church or community center where people go out of their way to extend hospitality and love to others during the holidays.

Next to family and friends, finances are a close second when deciding how we 'spend' the holidays. Alleviate some of this stress by budgeting carefully before you brave the malls or jump online.

Online shopping, when done carefully, can save you the hassles of holiday crowds. If you think Christmas is getting too commercial, why not try adopting a five or ten dollar gift policy? That means you only accept and give 5 or 10 dollar presents. This will make the holidays more about the people and less about the stuff, and is a cool protest against the shopping gods to boot.

A final tip for handling the holidays is to recognize that how you feel can be strongly influenced with your physical state. And sometimes it's a good idea to think twice before you decide on a second helping of cheesecake or yet another cocktail. Pace yourself over the holidays because if you don't you may not be able to keep your Christmas cheer for as long as you'd like. If you're too tired to go out, stay in. And if you "just can't eat another bite," don't feel pressured to stuff yourself. Regular exercise is, of course, always a good idea, but if the holidays are just too busy for you, why not start a routine in the New Year? Give yourself a gym pass for a Christmas present as motivation.

So have a blast during your holiday seasons, but don't overdo it. Remember that holidays like Christmas are soon over and you can choose to remember the holiday in one of two ways. The first is to make some great memories for you to recall throughout the year. The alternative makes for a less appealing reminder and comes in the form of about 15 extra pounds on the waistline and a credit card bill that just won't quit reminding you of your overindulgences. So let the sugarplums dance more in your head and less in your tummy.

Anxiety

All anxiety disorders affect behavior, thoughts, emotions, and physical health. It's common for a person to suffer from more than one disorder at the same time, or to also experience depression, eating disorders, and drugs and alcohol abuse along with the anxiety disorder. Here's a description of each of the major anxiety disorders:

Panic Disorder

Panic disorder is accompanied by panic attacks, and typically begins in a person's late teen years or early 20s. Agoraphobia is often coupled with panic disorder, and is the fear of being in places or situations perceived as difficult to escape from, or would be hard to receive help, should a panic attack occur. When a person has panic disorder with agoraphobia, they try extremely hard to avoid public situations. In some cases, people fear being alone, and in other cases, they refuse to be in public, sometimes staying at home for long periods.

Panic Attacks

A person with panic disorder regularly has panic attacks, which are marked by sudden feelings of terror and arise without warning. Feelings experienced during these attacks may include:

• Shortness of breath

- Chest pain
- Heart palpitations
- Choking or smothering sensations
- Dizziness or unsteadiness
- Tingling in extremities
- Hot and cold flashes
- Sweating
- Faintness
- Trembling and shaking
- Fear of dying, going crazy, or behaving uncontrollably during an attack
- Phobias

Phobias are classified as either social phobias or specific phobias. Social phobias, simply put, are fears about social situations. People with this type of phobia are exceptionally worried about doing something wrong in front of other people, and are self-conscious and afraid that they're being watched or observed. These feelings are paralyzing and irrational, but could be so extreme that they refuse to place themselves in situations where this social fear may arise.

Specific phobias also consist of involuntary, irrational fears, and common examples are fears of flying, heights, planes, elevators, and animals. These objects can induce such high levels of anxiety that their lives are significantly affected.

Generalized Anxiety Disorder

This type of anxiety is characterized by ongoing, repeated nervousness and worry about routine life activities and events. Physical symptoms include nausea, trembling, fatigue, muscle tension, and headaches. The source of the tension has no particular focus, and the person anticipates a worst case scenario.

Obsessive-Compulsive Disorder

A person who constantly washes their hands, checks to make sure the stove is turned off, or counts out an amount over and over again may have this disorder. OCD is characterized by persistent unwanted thoughts and rituals to deal with these thoughts. The person is concerned, doubtful, and disturbed.

Post-Traumatic Stress Disorder

Sometimes an event can be so terrifying that it can cause flashbacks - in which the person relives the experience - nightmares, depression, anger, and/or irritability, which are all symptoms of this disorder. Events that can trigger PTSD are ones in which serious harm occurred or was threatened, such as rape, child abuse, murder, worksite accidents, war or a natural disaster. In other words, any happening that threatens or creates loss of life.

It's understandable that you don't forget significant events over your lifetime, especially episodes that posed a threat to your well-being, those around you, or even your very life.

I can still recollect with startling clarity the time, many years ago, when I was trapped in a crashed vehicle, upside down, and not knowing whether I was going to survive or not.

I can also remember as if it was yesterday the tragic day six years ago when I found the body of a close friend who had committed suicide.

Yet, sometimes the experience can have such an impact, and be so unexpected, that some people simply aren't prepared to cope with the aftermath of such a shock to their system. Instead of moving on, the grief and other residual feelings remain, and manifest themselves in an anxiety disorder known as post-traumatic stress disorder (PTSD).

A variety of events, including rapes or muggings, accidents, military action, natural disasters, and witnessing a death, can trigger PTSD. These events, known as "stressors," can affect both children and adults, alone and in a group. Usually, PTSD symptoms begin within 3 months of when the event occurred, but it varies, from one person to another – as do the symptoms themselves.

However, at the same time, it may be years down the road before PTSD occurs. And for some, recovery may happen within 6 months, but for others, the process is much more gradual.

PTSD is often accompanied by other anxiety disorders, substance abuse, or physical illness. These accompanying maladies may serve to mask the existence of PTSD. PTSD, though, can be diagnosed and treated, and is characterized by three categories of symptoms. The first and main symptom is re-experiencing the event. Typically, this involves vivid flashbacks, or recurrent nightmares in which the experience is re-lived. Anniversaries, or similar situations, can be especially aggravating.

The second category involves avoidance and emotional numbing. A person may begin to withdraw from activities and stay away from situations where they can potentially be reminded of the traumatic event. Avoiding friends and family, as well as a loss of interest in previously enjoyed activities are also part of this category. In addition, a person may be numb to feeling emotions, in particular intimacy, or may feel tremendous guilt or enter a dissociative state, where they believe they are re- living the event.

The final category consists of increased alertness and changes in sleeping habits. It may be difficult for a person with PTSD to concentrate, complete tasks, or fall asleep.

PTSD, like other anxiety disorder treatment, is usually treated with a combination of medication and NeuroLinguistic Programming (NLP), or a proper PTSD workshop.

While traumatic events are unforgettable, they should not negatively affect and interfere with our daily activities and routines. Understanding post-traumatic stress disorder, its symptoms, and realizing that treatment is available, is an integral first step in placing the events where they belong - in our memories.

10 Practical Coping Strategies

1.   Don't worry about things that are out of your control (e.g., the weather.)

2.   Brace yourself for events you know will be stressful. Recognizing that stress is coming will increase your threshold and will give you time to take a different perspective on the situation.

3.   Work to resolve conflicts with other people. Once you resolve conflicts with friends and coworkers you'll be

able to communicate better, work more efficiently, and feel less anxious when you need their help.

4.   Ask for help from friends, family, and coworkers. Often these people want to help, are required to help, or are just being lazy by not offering help. Don't be a pushover and get suckered into doing everything yourself. Even if your son complains, chances are he doesn't really mind unloading those groceries for you.

5.   Set goals and make them realistic.

6.   Make time to do things that you enjoy, get away from your daily stresses. Social events, group sports, and hobbies are just a few ideas.

7.   Don't spread yourself too thin. Say NO if you don't have the time or energy to do something. Taking on another task when you're already maxed-out will not only cause you distress, but will also cause the quality of your work and play to suffer.

8.   View change as positive, not as a threat. As humans, we are designed to be highly adaptable, able to

adjust to all kinds of environments. Change is a healthy aspect of life from an evolutionary as well as a psychological perspective. Embrace change and look to discover new opportunities for personal growth and fulfillment.

9.　　Find out what works for you. Many self-help books and workshops have been written and created by reputable professionals. Take a look at some of these to learn specific strategies that will work for you.

10.　　Get professional help if you have to. A few sessions with a professional counselor may help you if your situation persists. Persistent problems in dealing with stress may indicate a deeper problem.

Anger

Humans have a wide range of emotions, and anger is a perfectly acceptable and common one. We all feel the need to address our frustrations, and to take quick action to alleviate our anger. But when do you know that anger is beyond your control and that you might have an anger management issue on your hands? Find out the warning signs, and what you can do about it. Also, if you're a parent, learn how to discern between clumsy and aggressive behavior in your child, and how you can deal with your child's temper tantrums.

Controlling Your Anger

Sure, everyone gets mad at some time or another. But what if all you could think about was 100 ways to get even with that "rat who snagged that promotion" you coveted? That could be a signal that anger is affecting your life more than you think. Learn about other warning signs and ways to help deal with your anger and rage.

Let's face it: everyone gets angry. Even real-life Paragons and other "saints-in- training" get irked by some events that trigger an upsetting or aggressive response. Most of us will get over it; time will pass, the world goes on, and tomorrow will be another day. But for others, anger can build up over time until it has the potential of reaching a dangerous and serious point.

Like any emotion, anger is normal. It helps the individual in dealing with a tense or troubling situation by offering an outlet of release. By the same token, however, too much of it bottled inside at the same time or blowing too much steam all at once, can turn anger from a healthy life management tool into an ugly problem that hurts you and those around you. If you're like that, read on to learn how to let the hot air out of that angry little kettle of yours. If you're not like that, you too should read on, because you might also one day reach a breaking point that will drive you bonkers.

While anger is normal, there are some symptoms that you should watch out for that may indicate that it is a life-interfering problem. First, you may have to address your anger if you can't get it off your mind before your rage consumes you and spills over into other things. Maybe you can't concentrate on getting that proposal in on the deadline because all you can think about is how some co-worker was such a self-centered inconsiderate jerk. Or all you talk about is how much you hate someone, and all that complaining is ruining your times with your friends and family.

Second, anger could be serious if it was caused by something that happened quite a while ago and you can't let go of it.

Third, if anger's causing you to plot and carry out vengeful plans that hurt others, you could be looking at a problem because of being obsessed with getting even. This isn't a mature way of handling things, and borders on the extreme. If you carry out your plans and become violent toward others, then your anger is leading you too far over the emotional cliff.

Too much or inappropriate anger can lead to serious detrimental effects. In terms of physical health, it can result in ulcers and heart disease. And with emotional well-being, it could affect your relationships with those around you, your career, and other important institutions in your life. But there are some strategies you can employ to help identify and resolve your anger during the actual moment, and some long-term guidelines that can assist you in approaching life in a calmer and more positive direction.

When anger happens, admit that you are angry, and release it - to an extent. Think moderation, and don't keep it bottled inside. Avoid overreaction by taking a step back.

Remove yourself from the situation and ask yourself if someone else in your place would be reacting in the same manner. Look at the situation, too; is it really that bad that it's worth getting all worked up about?

Try to think about something else when you feel that rush of anger. Hum a favorite song or recall a happy moment instead of giving some tailgating jerk the one-fingered salute via your rear view mirror.

Identify the source of your anger, and try to deal with him or her directly in a peaceful and productive manner. Also listen carefully to what others have to say, and wait until they're finished before you speak. It's amazing how words get misconstrued just by jumping in too soon. Allowing the few extra moments for the other person to finish also gives you time to absorb what is being said and formulate an appropriate response.

There are a number of actions you can take to help channel your anger from an unpredictable and volatile problem into a controlled response framed by a new, more relaxed attitude. For instance, avoid blaming yourself, even if you feel that it is your mistake and your mistake alone. Make the best of a bad situation and learn from the experience instead. Check out how other people have handled the same problem, especially if it's a situation beyond your control, such as a job lay-off. What coping mechanisms did they use?

Help release your anger and any residual tension by discovering outlets. Physical activities are a great way to blow off steam in a positive way, and give you time to calm down and assess your situation. Find other outlets, such as tai chi, yoga, keeping a journal, relaxation therapy, meditation and deep-breathing exercises. Get in touch with your funny bone and learn to laugh at yourself. Not everything has to be three-piece- suited serious. Laugh and loosen that necktie a bit. In terms of the people around you, learn to trust their abilities. Having faith in others takes a lot of tension and potential anger out of the equation. Also find those who you feel comfortable enough to confide in. They can provide support, a sympathetic ear, and a different perspective on your situation. And if you need more information, a wealth of resources, from books to community organizations to mental health associations, can provide more insight into anger and anger management techniques.

Anger doesn't have to stay inside. Nor does it have to translate into hurtful and vengeful actions. Learning to deal with anger as it happens and adopting some long-term strategies can go a long way in helping you manage the next time you feel your blood boiling. No matter your personality, everyone feels angry at some time or another. By following these suggestions, you can take control of anger before it controls you.

Tempers Flare When The Stakes Are High

Many people find that they get angrier with their partner than any other person. This doesn't happen because of a cruel twist of fate that has you paired with the one person that makes you the angriest, but rather because intimate relationships have so much more invested in them than virtually any other kind of relationship. When a marriage breaks up the repercussions are felt in virtually every aspect of both partners' lives, from finances to personal happiness.

Anger is a normal emotion and should not be suppressed. Emotions have a way of being released even when they're bottled up. An explosion of anger because you've been bottling it up is the last thing you want. Because anger within an intimate relationship is inevitable, learning to express and use this emotion is very important. The constructive use of anger requires some self-control. When you exert self-control and remember that you will likely resolve and overcome the conflict, this can help you see the light at the end of the tunnel. Use that advanced neo-cortex to resist the chimp-like urge to scream and throw things at your partner and communicate your feelings instead. Admit your angry feelings and use them as a doorway to communication rather than as an excuse to put the other person down.

Your angry feelings toward your partner can be a warning sign of something deeper that may be troubling you. Search your feelings to discover if your anger is a manifestation of hurt, fear, frustration, or feelings of inadequacy. Discovering and exploring these deeper feelings together with your partner can go a long way toward building intimacy.

Support Groups

Release some of your anger or help someone with an anger management problem by talking it out there. Who hasn't experienced a time when the only thing in the world that will make things better is some time alone and a good cry? These feelings usually go away after a short period, but in some cases, the self-blame, worthlessness, and emptiness linger for several weeks at a time, and sometimes even longer. Depression can become a serious illness.

Suicide

Why would anyone want to end his or her life? Although the reasons are as varied as the people who consider such a solution, the general shared sentiment is an extreme feeling of hopelessness, helplessness, and desperation towards a situation. Suicide is a final and permanent answer to a complex web of often temporary circumstances, and yet also serves as a cry for help.

Mourning Suicide

When a loved one commits suicide, those left behind to pick up the pieces not only have to cope with the loss of that person, but often with the complicated hurt that arises when we believe that our own behavior may have influenced another's choices.

It is not your fault.

Very often, friends and relatives of the deceased tend to blame themselves for the suicide. "If only…" becomes the lament of those left behind. "If only I had been a better friend." "If only I had been less self-absorbed and seen the pain he was in." "If only I had insisted he get help."

The truth of the matter is that you are not to blame. Nothing you could have done would have changed the outcome. Suicide is an individual decision. We are not responsible for the actions of others.

If you are experiencing feelings of guilt or responsibility for the loss of a loved one, seek help. Attend a support group or see a bereavement counselor. You don't have to go through this alone.

What Kind of Grief is Normal?

The short answer is that there is no one 'normal' reaction to the suicide of a loved one. Everyone deals with loss differently. That means that everything you are feeling right now is natural, even if you feel angry, or confused, or even relieved. In order to successfully deal with your grief you must work through your feelings, not deny them.

Stages to Look Out For

Though there may be no one way to grieve, there are stages that most people go through as they mourn. Initially, you may experience shock. You may feel numb, as though you are just going through the motions of your life. You may not want to talk about the death with others and may remove yourself emotionally from loved ones.

You may feel disorganized, as if your life has just been turned upside down. You may feel lonely and depressed and you may cry unexpectedly. Maybe your appetite has decreased, and you can't seem to sleep. It may be helpful if you talk to someone about how you are feeling at this point.

Once you have started talking about your feelings, you may begin to reorganize your life. There may be moments when you don't think about the loss at all. You are more able to cope with daily tasks, and encouragement from loved ones only makes you stronger. As you work through the painful emotions that are the grieving process, you are learning to live with your loss, lessening the chance that you will be consumed by it. And remember, we all grief in different ways and we heal at different rates. You can't rush it.

STRESS MANAGEMENT

Introduction

Stress is a part of day to day living. As college students you may experience stress meeting academic demands, adjusting to a new living environment, or developing friendships. The stress you experience is not necessarily harmful. Mild forms of stress can act as a motivator and energizer. However, if your stress level is too high, medical and social problems can result.

What is Stress?

Although we tend to think of stress as caused by external events, events in themselves are not stressful. Rather, it is the way in which we interpret and react to events that makes them stressful. People differ dramatically in the type of events they interpret as stressful and the way in which they respond to such stress. For example, speaking in public can be stressful for some people and relaxing for others.

Symptoms of Stress

There are several signs and symptoms that you may notice when you are experiencing stress. These signs and symptoms fall into four categories: Feelings, Thoughts, Behavior, and Physiology. When you are under stress, you may experience one or more of the following:

- Low self-esteem.
- Fear of failure.
- Inability to concentrate.
- Embarrassing easily.
- Worrying about the future.

Thoughts

- Preoccupation with thoughts/tasks.
- Forgetfulness.
- Feeling anxious.
- Feeling scared.

- Feeling irritable.
- Feeling moody.

Feelings

- Feeling anxious.
- Feeling scared.
- Feeling irritable.
- Feeling moody

Behavior

- Stuttering and other speech difficulties.
- Crying for no apparent reason.
- Acting impulsively.
- Startling easily.
- Laughing in a high pitch and nervous tone of voice.
- Grinding your teeth.
- Increasing smoking.
- Increasing use of drugs and alcohol.
- Being accident prone.
- Losing your appetite or overeating.

- Perspiration /sweaty hands.
- Increased heartbeat.
- Trembling.
- Nervous ticks.
- Dryness of throat and mouth.
- Tiring easily.
- Urinating frequently

Physiology

- Sleeping problems / poor quality of sleep.
- Diarrhea / indigestion / vomiting.
- Butterflies in stomach.
- Headaches.
- Premenstrual tension.
- Pain in the neck and or lower back.
- Loss of appetite or overeating.
- Susceptibility to illness.

Causes of Stress

Both positive and negative events in one's life can be stressful. However, major life changes are the greatest contributors of stress for most people. They place the greatest demand on resources for coping.

Major Life Changes That Can Be Stressful

- Geographic mobility.
- Going to college / transfer to a new school.
- Marriage.
- Pregnancy.
- New job.
- New life style.
- Divorce.
- Financial insecurity.
- Death of a loved one.
- Being fired from your job.

Environmental Changes That Can Be Stressful

- Time pressure.
- Competition.
- Financial problems.
- Noise.
- Disappointments.

How to Reduce Stress

Many stresses can be changed, eliminated, or minimized. Here are some things you can do to reduce your level of stress:

- Become aware of your own reactions to stress.
- Reinforce positive self-statements.
- Focus on your good qualities and accomplishments.
- Avoid unnecessary competition.
- Develop assertive behaviors.
- Recognize and accept your limits. Remember that everyone is unique and different.
- Get a hobby or two. Relax and have fun.
- Exercise regularly.
- Eat a balanced diet daily.
- Talk with friends or someone you can trust about your worries/problems.
- Learn to use your time wisely:
  - Evaluate how you are budgeting your time.
  - Plan ahead and avoid procrastination.

- o   Make a weekly schedule and try to follow it.
- Set realistic goals.
- Set priorities.
- When studying for an exam, study in short blocks and gradually lengthen the time you spend studying. Take frequent short breaks.
- Practice relaxation techniques. For example, whenever you feel tense, slowly breathe in and out for several minutes.

WHAT DOES IT MEAN TO BE SUICIDAL?

You may be ill.

You may be desperate.

You look in a thick text-book of psychology and there is no description of you. The topic of suicide is spread throughout the whole text - you can't read it all, and even if you could, it wouldn't help.

If you are ill, you must get help.

If you are desperate, you should also get some help. Suicidal thinking is potentially very serious but it is not very specific and it can be very common.

Many people who are suicidal cannot find the words to express their feelings. They feel trapped and do not know how to get out.

The most important thing for a suicidal individual to do is to stay connected to their families, friends, support systems, and the people they love and care about. If they stay connected, they can work out their feelings over time.

Some Medical Considerations

You may be at serious risk of suicide.

- if you are on the cusp of a serious breakdown as a young adult
- if you have a severe depression and you are in treatment and you are getting better on the outside and you have a lot of energy now but you still feel horrible on the inside
- if you have lost your wife and your children and your job and your family support because they love your wife more than they love you and you

have a depression and you are spending a lot of time alone and you are a drinker

- if you are old now and have lost your spouse and you are medically ill and you do not feel valued and you have nothing to do
- if you have a loved one who committed suicide and you are like that person or you have a similar condition and you believe that like them you will never get better

Suicidal thinking is not a specific symptom. It may point concern in any number of directions. Sorting it out requires you to sort out the underlying factors.

If You Are Suicidal: Please Don't Drink

You are thinking of ending your life. You have arranged to be alone with a bottle of liquor on a Saturday night. You are listening to your favorite music. You know where your family and friends are - not with you.

Drinking increases the risk of trouble for a number of reasons.

- you will feel better before you feel worse and you desperately want to feel better
- you will think you will feel even better if you drink more, so you keep going
- eventually you are more likely to do something impulsive and dangerous and destructive
- you will lose your ability to delay frustration
- you will forget what little you do remember to help yourself
- you will believe your pain will never go away
- you will feel guilty because you know that you have blown it by drinking
- you will forget what medicines you have taken or how much you have been drinking, and you will redouble your efforts with dangerous consequences

A high percentage of suicides are associated with substance abuse and alcoholism.

It is a bad statistical group to be in.

If You Are Suicidal: Your Thoughts Are All Mixed Up Together

If you are suicidal, it is possible that you are not really getting to your thoughts.
The suicidal thinking may be a final common pathway for the brain when it overloads and you cannot find answers to your questions.

Here is a situation.

- you are angry at your parents for not helping you out more
- you are angry at your girlfriend for not realizing how you need her to be supportive
- you are depressed and you are having trouble getting the words out
- if you could get the words out, you do not know how you will be received because you are already sad.
- you are trapped, behind in your school, behind in your work, behind in your finances
- you don't know where to start to begin speaking
- you do not know who to start speaking to

- you do not know how to get your life started. It seems to be stuck

Suicidal thoughts are often a mixture of other thoughts that are camouflaged. When you can track backwards and fine those other thoughts, you may experience relief.

If You Are Suicidal: Another Example

You are at the end of your rope.

- your boyfriend is bad news and you have rejected him, but you cannot pay the rent on your own.
- your best friend is a good support, but she is out of town. Your mother is one of your closest friends but you are afraid that she will be disappointed in you when she finds out that you cannot cope.
- you want help but you do not want to talk to a counselor.

What you want is impossible.

- you cannot reject your boyfriend and have him pay the rent.
- you cannot talk to your girlfriend if you cannot find her.
- you cannot gain support from a family member or a counselor unless you speak to them honestly.

Sometimes suicidal thinking is due to wanting something impossible. In this situation, it may help to find out what is impossible in your thinking. Once you have done that, there will be emotional work to do. You will know who to connect with, who to speak with, what to say.

If You Are Suicidal: Some Medical Thoughts

Suicide is sometimes a medical emergency.

When someone suicidal is seen in an emergency situation, they often need two basic things:

1. they need help to calm themselves down
2. they need to connect with someone for help

Many strategies can help calm someone down.

These may include bringing in supports, talking out the problem if they are up to it, taking charge for the person temporarily while expecting them to pick up the pieces later, taking them out of the crisis, loaning them money, giving them medicine that will calm them. If this is not happening, call the crisis line or go to a hospital and ask for direction.

Connecting with someone for help generates realistic hope.

- Clinical problems need to be treated.
- Conflicts need to be resolved.
- Financial problems need to be fixed.
- Fuzzy thinking needs to be cleared up.

You harm yourself because you feel guilty and deserve to be hurt.

Some Suicide-Like Behaviors

You cut yourself with a knife.

You take too many pills to get to sleep, to calm down, to upset your loved ones.

You cut yourself with a knife to obtain relief from your agitation, to bring your pain out into the open, to make your pain real, to relieve your desire to harm yourself in worse ways.

You take too many pills to finally get some relief, to knock yourself out, to let everybody know that you are suffering and nothing seems to be working.

You harm yourself because you feel guilty and deserve to be hurt.

Sometimes, harming yourself in some of these ways carries a mixed message. It often relieves physical tension. It often also represents different threads of meaning. You are trying to harm yourself. You are trying to alleviate your pain. You are trying to communicate your suffering. You are trying to absolve yourself of guilt. You are trying to get help. You are trying to avoid getting help. Sorting out the underlying meaning of the behaviors can be life-saving.

Sorting Out Suicide-Like Behaviors

You cut yourself or hurt yourself in some way. If this is
happening, there are two things you need to know.

1.   You need to know the clinical reason.
2.   You need to know the emotional reason.

There is usually both a clinical reason and an emotional
reason. You have to figure them both out.

The clinical reason is often that you are depressed.

The emotional reason has to do with the meaning behind
what you are doing. The way you harm yourself may be
very personal; it may include a number of meaningful
emotions camouflaged into one destructive behavior.

- if you have lost hope, generate hope
- if you are punishing yourself, work on self esteem
- if you are guilty, find out what you have done
  wrong learn to communicate your feelings
- get your needs met in more direct ways
- work out your conflicts
- find out what you want from people

- find out what the self-destructive behavior really means. If you find it out, the pressure towards self harm will diffuse.

Signs

- appetite fluctuations
- apathy
- sleep habit changes
- low self-esteem
- "down" attitude
- suicide ideation
- lack of concentration
- withdrawal
- irritability
- substance abuse

Breakdown of Statistics

Total suicides in 2005	= 36,019	
under 20 yrs	= 3,062	= 8.5%
20 – 24 yrs	= 2,882	= 8%
25 – 44 yrs	= 15,128	= 42%
45 – 64 yrs	= 10,517	= 29.2%
65 + yrs	= 4,430	= 12.3%

NOTE: the quoted statistics are Canada and USA numbers combined.

Sexual Breakdown Under 20

- total suicides under 20   =   312
- male   = 246   = 78.8%
- female =   66   = 21.2%

DEPRESSION

People can't be happy all the time. Sadness is a natural response to life's problems and misfortunes.

Who hasn't experienced a time when the only thing in the world that will make things better is some time alone and a good cry? Fortunately, these feelings usually go away after a short period, but in some cases, the self-blame, worthlessness, and emptiness linger for several weeks at a time, and sometimes even longer.

Depression can become a serious illness. Learn more about depression and what causes it. If you believe that you might be depressed, discover signs to watch out for and the treatment methods available. If you suspect that someone is depressed, find out what you can do to help. It's not a simple matter of feeling blue. It's a very personal concern that needs your compassion and awareness.

Depression: How You Can Help

The support of family and friends is immeasurable in assisting to help those people with depression. Some people who are depressed usually keep to themselves, while others fear being alone. Regardless of the way in which they wish to carry on, you can help by being patient and reassuring.

Grieving

It's our typical response to a loss in our lives – be it a loved one, a way of life, or our health. We grieve not for the loss itself, but for what that loss means to us. Here's where you can examine the kinds of changes personal loss can bring.

Support Groups

The support of family and friends is immeasurable in assisting to help those people with depression. Some people who are depressed usually keep to themselves, while others fear being alone. Regardless of the way in which they wish to carry on, you can help by being patient and reassuring. Sometimes it's frustrating and difficult to understand why a depressed person is feeling so down and can't snap out of it. With your understanding you can do your best to assist him or her. Above all else, people with depression need you to be a supportive, steadying influence.

Some Things to Keep in Mind

- Don't jump to conclusions.
- Look for changes during treatment. You will often notice an initial improvement in the depressed person's condition which he or she may first be unaware of.
- Be a good listener. You don't always have to have the answers. Be available, and let them talk without interrupting.
- Avoid criticism as it could lead to further feelings of guilt and worthlessness.
- Avoid over pampering or babying them.

- Maintain an even temper. You need to be patient because they're often irritable and short with their temper.

- Do not feel guilty or responsible for their condition. They need your support, but if you believe you're to blame, you won't be in the best position to assist them.

- Share the responsibility. Depression is an incredible weight to carry on your own. Find other friends, family, doctors, and organizations that can lend a hand.

- Carry on with your own life. Do not put it on hold while trying to take care of a depressed person.

- Take care of your own health. If you don't practice proper eating, sleeping, and exercise habits, your personal wellness could suffer, and so could your abilities to help them.

- Keep everything in balance as much as possible. They need stability, but do not give up your own life trying to do so. They need support, but do not take their lives over for them. It involves walking a fine line, but the help you'll give them will be immeasurable.

Depression Primer

People speak all the time about being depressed. They've had a bad day at work, fought with their significant other, or their beloved goldfish passed away. Most of the times, these episodes of sadness are temporary and short-lived. But for others, the feeling of "being down" lingers, and it requires quite some time and effort to bring themselves back up.

It's estimated that 15% of the population will experience a major depressive episode at some point in their lives, but fortunately, depression is the most treatable mental illness. It is considered a mental illness when it is out of proportion to the event that caused it, lasts long after the event is over, has no apparent cause, or seriously interferes with routine activities.

No one knows what exactly causes depression. Contrary to popular belief, it's not just a state of mind that is out of control. More likely it's a combination of several factors. The most common belief is that it is a chemical imbalance in one or more neurotransmitters, which are responsible for transmitting information across your brain pathways. Another factor that often comes into play is a specific, distressing life event such as a death in the family or a job layoff. Psychological factors, like a negative or pessimistic view of life, may also make people more susceptible. As well, a person with a family history of the condition is more prone to experiencing depression. And once a person has had depression, he or she is more likely to be depressed again.

The good news is that depression is rarely permanent, and with professional treatment, it can end a lot sooner. Knowing the warning signs to watch out for is the first step in conquering the illness.

Signs

But if after a few weeks of self-help nothing has changed, you should consult professional help. Depression is very treatable, and there are many methods available that can help to bring about changes for the better. Remember too, that time helps to alleviate the feelings of sadness brought about by depression. But if after a few weeks of self-help, you should consult professional help. Here are some suggestions to help yourself:

- Make life more manageable by breaking down larger projects into smaller tasks.
- Take them on one at a time.
- Write out a list of goals for each day, and check them off as they're completed.
- Be proud when you have made an accomplishment, and don't berate yourself for not getting as much done as you would have liked to.
- Find some outlets. Physical exercise is great, as well as time spent with family and friends.
- Set aside time for yourself each day, for the things that you like to do.
- Put off making important life decisions.
- If you are on prescribed medications, remember to take them regularly, and report any side effects to your doctor.
- Avoid alcohol, which is a depressant.

Following these guidelines can greatly help in overcoming depression. Other times, though, these methods alone may not be enough or the depression may last for a prolonged period, and your doctor may recommend treatment instead of time and self- help methods in these cases. The two main types of treatment are medications and psychotherapies. These methods, along with the support of family, friends, and self-help groups can also help people who are suffering from depression to lead full and active lives.

Medications, or drug treatment, are used by physicians to correct the chemical imbalance in the brain that is responsible for bringing about the depression. Contrary to popular belief, these drugs are not tranquilizers, uppers, or downers. Neither are they addictive. Results are usually apparent after a few weeks. There are a variety of drugs available, and your doctor can determine which is most appropriate for your situation.

Short-term solution-focused psychotherapies, or talk therapies – like NLP – are effective in treating depression. For people with long-term lifestyle or psychological attitudinal problems that may contribute to recurring episodes of depression, longer term psychotherapy may be necessary. These attitudes may also not be severe enough to lead to official clinical depression, but can still lead to negative feelings for the person.

Psychotherapy is also useful for long-term programs once the depression is over, and a perspective in lifestyle needs to be worked at on an ongoing basis to elicit positive change.

MIND AND BODY

Total health is not just about being free of disease. Our Dynamic Discovery view of health and well-being combines emotional health, psychological health, and spiritual health with physical health.

Wellness

Wellness means taking responsibility for your own well-being. That means always being aware of what contributes to your overall health, and choosing and acting accordingly. It means continually paying attention to all parts of your being, and taking action to ensure that you are doing what needs to be done physically, emotionally, and spiritually to be well.

The Importance of Staying Hydrated

How much water should you drink?

The general rule is eight glasses of water a day for the average adult. That number should be increased for individuals exercising, living or working in a hot environment, or who perspire more heavily.

PERSONAL SAFETY

You don't have to act or dress a certain way to have your personal safety threatened. Trust your instincts. If you feel like you're being harassed, you probably are. Recognize when a situation is dangerous, and discover how you can take action to increase your personal safety.

Am I Being Stalked?

It can be easy to confuse love with harassment. A person who pays a lot of attention to you, by calling you constantly and keeping tabs on you, and places you essentially at the center of their universe obviously cares a lot about you. Or do they? While it's natural to worry and to occupy a privileged position in certain people's lives, harassers take it too far.

It's a dangerous world out there. Keeping ourselves and our loved ones safe is often at the forefront of our minds. Learn how others are dealing with issues like stalking and assault.

AGING

It's inevitable. It happens to everyone. It's fraught with many life changes. It can sometimes seem like things are heading downhill and tumbling out of control.

But aging doesn't have to seize you, your vitality, and the decisions you make.

Granted, a lot of events occur as we get older - our physical strength is not as great as before, children leave home, loved ones pass away, retirement occurs, and there's a bigger chance of being lonely.

You can cope with these changes. You can draw on the support and strength of others, as well as prepare yourself for these events by adapting a long-term lifestyle that optimizes your emotional and physical well being. At the heart of this is plan is to maintain an interest in your life, and to stay active with people and pastimes that mean the most to you.

Dealing With Changes as We Get Older

Changes associated with aging can be grouped into four main categories: physical, losing loved ones, loneliness, and retirement. Each of these serves as an opportunity for you to strengthen your resolve and invoke positive lifestyle changes. By adopting some of these coping strategies, you can maintain an interest in your life and take control of the aging process so that aging and its changes, no matter how inevitable they seem, cannot grab a hold of you.

When we age we face many changes. Our bodies begin to slow down, our values may change, we may face the loss of loved ones or we may worry about being alone in our retirement. Find others who are experiencing the same.

PERSONAL LIFE EVENT ANALYSIS

To learn the level of stress (distress) in your life, *circle* the value at the right of each of the events on the following pages if it has occurred within the past 12 months:

Event	Value
Death of spouse	100
Divorce	73
Marital separation	65
Jail term	63
Death of close family member	63
Personal injury or illness	53
Marriage	50
Fired from job	47
Marital reconciliation	45

Event	Value
Retirement	45
Change in family member's health	44
Pregnancy	40
Sexual difficulties	39
Addition to family	39
Business readjustment	39
Change in financial status	38
Death of close friend	37
Career change	36
Change in number of marital arguments	35
Mortgage or loan over $10,000	31
Foreclosure of mortgage or loan	30
Change in work responsibilities	29
Son or daughter leaving home	29
Trouble with in-laws	29
Outstanding personal achievement	28
Spouse begins or ceases working	26
Starting or finishing school	26
Change in living conditions	25
Revision of personal habits	24
Trouble with boss	23
Change in work hours, conditions	20
Change in residence	20

Event	Value
Change in schools	20
Change in recreational habits	19
Change in church activities	19
Change in social activities	18
Mortgage or loan under $10,000	17
Change in sleeping habits	16
Change in number of family gatherings	15
Change in eating habits	15
Vacation	13
Christmas season	12
Minor violation of the law	11

How to Analyze Your Score*

Add the circled values. If your total score is more than 150, find ways to reduce stress in your daily life so that your stress level doesn't increase. The higher the score, the harder one needs to work at staying physically well.

Suggested Use For Personal Life Events Analysis

1.   Become familiar with the different events and the amounts of stress they promote.

2.   Put the list of events where your family can easily refer to it several times a day.

3.   Practice recognizing the stress level when one of these events happens.

4.   Think about the meaning of the event for you and identify your feelings.

5.   Think about the different ways you can adjust to the event.

6.   Take your time in arriving at decisions.

7.   Anticipate life changes and plan for them well in advance whenever possible.

8.   Pace yourself. It can be done even if you are in a hurry.

9.   Look at the accomplishment of a task as a part of ongoing daily living; avoid looking at such an achievement as a stopping point. Congratulate yourself and push ahead.

10.   Recognize that your internal mechanism of coping with stress is directly tied to how your health and well being will be influenced by it.

*This scale is derived from the Holmes-Rahe Social Readjustment Scale. Holmes,
& Rahe, R. (1967) "Holmes-Rahe Social Readjustment Rating Scale", Journal of Psychosomatic Research, vol. II.

PREVENTING STRESS BY LIVING A BALANCED LIFE

You'd Better Eat Your Vegetables…

Living a balanced life includes eating well, exercising regularly, sleeping enough, and not abusing drugs and alcohol… no small feat. Eating well means learning about nutrition so you're aware of what's healthy and what's not. Also, you may end up spending more time and money on food that doesn't taste quite as good as you try and cook (and buy) healthier meals.

Get That Butt in Gear…

Exercising regularly will help you raise your metabolism and achieve greater physical fitness. This will leave you with more energy to seize the day with and will give you some time to spend on yourself.

Deal With Your Problems…

Unless you do, they're not going anywhere. Whether they're related to work, relationships, anger, communication, anxiety, family members or friends, dealing with your problems promptly just makes good sense. This way they won't accumulate to the point that they overwhelm you. This doesn't mean that you should dwell on your problems. Nothing will make you feel worse than wallowing in your own self-pity. Once you identify a plan of action, let it ride and do something fun.

That Glass is Half Full!

Having a positive attitude is good advice for anyone. Once positive thinking becomes a habit for you, you'll find yourself identifying solutions instead of worrying yourself sick. Being positive will help your social life as well; your family and friends will appreciate it.

RELAXATION TRAINING

Start by choosing a muscle and holding it tight for a fw seconds. Many people find it helps to start with the muscles of the feet working up to the facial muscles. Relax the muscle after a few seconds. Do this with all of your muscles if they're all healthy. If you're pregnant DO NOT contract any abdominal muscles.

Stretching

If your neck and shoulders are healthy, try rolling your head in a gentle circle. Reach toward the ceiling and bend side to side slowly. Roll your shoulders. All of these things can help you relax.

Meditation

Meditation can effectively help reduce psychological stress. Although visions of the Maharishi-cross-legged and chanting-may pop into your head at the thought of meditating, this technique is not as mystical as it's cracked up to be. Meditating can effectively help reduce psychological stress. The key is to not stop yourself from thinking about things while trying not to focus on any one thing for too long. Let your thoughts flow down a peaceful river of dreams... how cerebral.

Deep Relaxed Breathing

This technique goes well with meditation and is easily accomplished in 5 simple steps.

1.   Lie down on a flat surface.
2.   Place one hand on your stomach, just above your navel and the other on your chest.
3.   Breathe in through your nose slowly and try to make your stomach rise a little.
4.   Hold your breath for a second.

5.   Breathe out through your nose slowly and let your stomach go back down.

•   Don't worry about things that are out of your control (e.g., the weather.)

•   Brace yourself for events you know will be stressful. Recognizing that stress is coming will increase your threshold and will give you time to take a different perspective on the situation.

•   Work to resolve conflicts with other people. Once you resolve conflicts with friends and coworkers you'll be able to communicate better, work more efficiently, and feel less anxious when you need their help.

•   Ask for help from friends, family, and co-workers. Often these people want to help, are required to help, or are just being lazy by not offering help. Don't be a pushover and get suckered into doing everything yourself. Even if your son complains, chances are he doesn't really mind unloading those groceries for you.

•   Set goals and make them realistic.

• Make time to do things that you enjoy, get away from your daily stresses. Social events, group sports, and hobbies are just a few ideas.

• Don't spread yourself too thin. Say NO if you don't have the time or energy to do something. Taking on another task when you're already maxed-out will not only cause you distress, but will also cause the quality of your work and play to suffer.

• View change as positive, not as a threat. As humans, we are designed to be highly adaptable, able to adjust to all kinds of environments. Change is a healthy aspect of life from an evolutionary as well as a psychological perspective.

• Embrace change and look to discover new opportunities for personal growth and fulfillment.

• Find out what works for you. Many self-help books and workshops have been written and created by reputable professionals. Take a look at some of these to learn specific strategies that will work for you.

•   Get professional help if you have to. A few
sessions with a professional counselor may help you if
your situation persists. Persistent problems in dealing
with stress may indicate a deeper problem.

Relaxation Techniques

Learning to Relax
You may have grown to accept a certain high level of
stress and anxiety as "normal". You may be unfamiliar
with what it feels like to be relaxed, calm, and unstressed.
With progressive relaxation you learn what it feels like to
be relaxed, you learn to increase relaxation to a new
level. By doing this you not only improve your physical
wellbeing by reducing hypertension, headaches, and other
physical complaints, but you improve your mental state
by reducing stress, anxiety, irritability, and depression.

The Physical Setting

Progressive relaxation should take place in a quiet,
attractive room. You should be completely supported.
There should be no need for exertion to maintain body

support. You should wear comfortable, loose fitting clothing during the sessions.

The Process

Lie on the floor or a bed and follow the directions of the relaxation technique as you tense and relax various muscle groups. After the initial tensing of the muscles, release the tension instantly and completely. This is very important in order to get the "pendulum effect". The muscles relax beyond the point of their normal relaxed state. You should then feel the important difference between tension and relaxation. You should concentrate on the feeling of relaxation, learn what it is to relax and how to increase it. Continually repeat to yourself, "Know what it feels like to be relaxed, deepen the relaxation, and know what it is to be relaxed."

"Do's" and "Don'ts" of Relaxation

Do: Make sure you have comfortable, loose clothing and proper back support

Don't: Put yourself in an awkward position or in a position that will make it easy to fall asleep

Do: Allow your mind to quiet down. If tense thoughts enter while you are relaxing, let them pass out of your head.

Don't: Think your way into tension. If you can't clear your mind, take a long, deep breath and let it out slowly.

Do: Stay alert and conscious while you are relaxing. Pay close attention and note any changes in your body (feelings that stand out for you).

Don't: Allow yourself to become groggy and sleepy. If you start falling asleep, open your eyes and sit up. When you are ready, return to relaxation posture.

Do: Go at your own pace and let go of your muscles as your body decides to give up tension.

Don't: Expect yourself to relax all at once. Like any other physical exercise, you must practice letting go step by step.

Do: Give your body messages of appreciation for relaxing as you notice these feelings going through your body.

Don't: Get down on yourself for not relaxing. Your body should be trusted to go at its own pace.

Do: Stay aware of your breathing. Observe how much air you're taking in full breaths at regular rhythms.

Don't: Smoke before, during or after relaxation as it tightens lung tissue and blood vessels. Let your body breathe.

Record these directions for yourself by reading them slowly.

Settle back as comfortably as you can and close your eyes. Let yourself relax to the best of your ability. Now, as you relax like that, clench your right fist. Just clench your fist tighter and tighter and study the tension as you do so. Keep it clenched and feel the tension in your right fist, hand, and forearm. Now relax. Let the fingers of your right hand become loose, and observe the contrast in your feelings. Now, let yourself go and try to become more relaxed all over. Once more, clench your right fist really tight Y hold it, and notice the tension again. Now let go, relax; your fingers straighten out and you notice the difference once more. Repeat that with your left fist. Clench your left fist while the rest of your body relaxes; clench that fist tighter and feel the tension. Now relax. Again, enjoy the contrast. Repeat that once more. Clench the left fist, tight and tense. Now do the opposite of tension: relax and feel the difference. Continue relaxing like that for a while. Clench both fists tighter and tighter, both fists tense, forearms tense. Study the sensations. Relax; straighten out your fingers and feel the relaxation. Continue relaxing your hands and forearms more and more.

Now bend your elbows and tense your biceps, tense them harder and study the tension feelings. All right. Straighten out your arms, let them relax and feel that difference again. Let the relaxation develop. Once more, tense your biceps; hold the tension and observe it carefully. Straighten the arms and relax; relax to the best of your ability. Each time, pay close attention to your feelings when you tense up and when you relax. Now straighten your arms. Straighten them so that you feel the most tension in the triceps muscles along the backs of your arms; stretch your arms and feel that tension. Now relax. Get your arms back into a comfortable position. Let the relaxation proceed on its own. The arms should feel comfortably heavy as you allow them to relax. Straighten the arms once more so that you feel the tension in the triceps muscles; straighten them. Feel that tension and relax. Now concentrate on pure relaxation in the arms without any tension. Get your arms comfortable and let them relax further and further. Continue relaxing your arms even further. Even when your arms seem fully relaxed, try to go that extra bit further; try to achieve deeper and deeper levels of relaxation.

Let all your muscles go loose and heavy. Just settle back quietly and comfortably. Wrinkle up your forehead now; wrinkle it tighter. Now, stop wrinkling your forehead; relax and smooth it out. Picture the entire forehead and scalp becoming smoother as the relaxation increased. Now, frown and crease your brows and study the tension. Let go of the tension again. Smooth out the forehead once more. Now, close your eyes tighter and tighter. Feel the tension. Relax your eyes. Keep your eyes closed, gently and comfortably, and notice the relaxation. Now clench your jaws, bite your teeth together; study the tension throughout the jaws. Relax your jaws now. Let your lips part slightly. Appreciate the relaxation. Now press your tongue hard against the roof of your mouth. Look for the tension. Alright. Let your tongue return to a comfortable and relaxed position. Now purse your lips. Press your lips together tighter and tighter. Relax the lips. Note the contrast between tension and relaxation. Feel the relaxation all over your face, all over your forehead and scalp, eyes, jaws, lips, tongue and throat. The relaxation progresses further and further.

Now attend to your neck muscles. Press your head back as far as it can go and feel the tension in the neck now roll it to the left. Straighten your head and bring it forward. Press your chin against your chest. Let your head return to a comfortable position and study the relaxation. Let the relaxation develop. Shrug your shoulders. Hold the tension. Drop your shoulders and feel the relaxation. Neck and shoulders relaxed. Shrug your shoulders again and move them around. Bring your shoulders up and forward and back. Feel the tension in your shoulders and in your upper back. Drop your shoulders once more and relax. Let the relaxation spread deep into the shoulders, right into your back muscles; relax your neck and throat, and your jaws and other facial areas as the pure relaxation takes over and grows deeper, deeper, ever deeper.

Relax your entire body to the best of your ability. Feel that comfortable heaviness that accompanies relaxation. Breathe easily and freely in and out. Notice how the relaxation increase as you exhale. As you breathe out, just feel that relaxation. Now breathe right in and fill your lungs inhale deeply and hold your breathe. Study the tension. Now exhale, let the walls of your chest grow loose and push the air out automatically. Continue relaxing and breathe freely, gently. Feel the relaxation and enjoy it. With the rest of your body as relaxed as possible, fill your lungs again. Breathe in deeply and hold it again. That's fine, breathe out and appreciate the relief. Just breathe normally. Continue relaxing your chest and let the relaxation spread to your back, shoulders, neck and arms. Merely let go. Enjoy the relaxation.

Now let's pay attention to your abdominal muscles; your stomach area. Tighten your stomach muscles, make your abdomen hard. Notice the tension. And relax. Let the muscles loosen and notice the contrast. Once more, press and tighten your stomach muscles, make your abdomen hard. Notice the tension. And relax. Let the muscles loosen and notice the contrast. Once more, press and tighten your stomach muscles. Hold the tension and study it, relax. Notice the general wellbeing that comes with relaxing your stomach. Now draw your stomach in, pull the muscles in and feel the tension this way.

Relax again, let your stomach out. Continue breathing normally and easily. Feel the gentle massaging action all over your chest and stomach. Now pull your stomach in again and hold the tension. Push out and tense like that; hold the tension. Once more, pull in and feel the tension.

Now relax your stomach fully. Let the tension dissolve as the relaxation grows deeper. Each time you breathe out, notice the rhythmic relaxation both in your lungs and in your stomach. Try and let go of all contractions anywhere in your body. Now direct your attention to your lower back. Arch your back, making your lower back quite hollow, and feel the tension along your spine. Settle down comfortably again, relaxing the lower   back. Just arch your back and feel the tension as you do so. Try to keep the ready of your body as relaxed as possible. Try to localize the tension throughout your lower back area. Relax once more, relaxing further and further. Relax your lower back, relax your upper back. Spread the relaxation to your stomach, chest, shoulders, arms and facial area, these parts relaxing further, further, further, ever deeper. Let go of all tensions and relax. Now flex your buttocks and thighs. Flex your thighs by pressing down your heels as hard as you can. Relax and note the difference. Straighten your knees and flex your thigh muscles again. Hold the tension. Relax your hips and thighs. Allow the relaxation to proceed on its own. Press your feet and toes downward, away from your face, so that your calf muscles become tense. Study the tension. Relax your feet and calves. This time, bend your feet toward your face so that you feel tension along your shins. Bring your toes right up. Relax again. Keep relaxing for a while.

Now let yourself relax further all over. Relax your feet, ankles, calves and shins, knees, thighs, buttocks and hips. Feel the heaviness of your lower body as you relax still further. Now spread the relaxation to your stomach, waist, and lower back. Let go more and more.

Feel that relaxation all over. Let it proceed to your upper back, chest, shoulders and arms, right to the tips of your fingers. Keep relaxing more and more deeply. Make sure that no tension has crept into your throat; relax your neck and your jaws and all your facial muscles. Keep relaxing your whole body like that for a while. Let yourself relax all over.

Now you can become twice as relaxed as you are merely by taking in a deep breath and exhaling slowly. With your eyes closed you become less aware of objects and movements around you, thus preventing any surface tensions from developing. Breathe in deeply and feel yourself becoming heavier. Take in a long, deep breath and let it out very slowly. Feel how heavy and relaxed you have become.

In a state of perfect relaxation you should feel unwilling to move a single muscle in your body. Think about the effort that would be required to raise your right arm. As you think about raising your right arm, see if you can notice any tensions that might have crept into your shoulder and arm. You decide not to lift the arm but to continue relaxing. Observe the relief and the disappearance of tension.

Just carry on relaxing like that. When you wish to get up, count backward from four to one. You should then feel fine, refreshed, wide awake and calm.

A Full Breathing Exercise

Step 1: Lie prone on the floor. Loosen your belt and restrictive clothing.

Step 2: Relax and exhale as completely as possible. Begin to inhale slowly making your belly rise. Now move your rib cage. Now your chest. Hold it for a second. Now, exhale completely, all the air out of your lungs. Try it again. This is complete breathing. Breathe normally for a while, and in the next minute take at least one more complete breath.
Pause one minute.

Step 3: You are still lying prone. As you lie there you will begin stretching muscles to achieve unblocked circulation. Bring your arms above your head and stretch them away from you fully. Now stretch your legs and feet downward, away from you, take a deep breath, let go and relax. Pause ten seconds. Feel the effects of the stretch on your body and on your breathing. Pause 15 seconds. Now sit up very slowly.

Step 4: Stand up for this part of the exercise. There are three very basic stretching postures to increase flexibility.

- backward bend
- forward bend
- side-to-side bend

As you do your backward bend pay attention to stretching your abdomen and back muscles. Important: Go only as far as you can. Don't push yourself. Bend slowly. As you do your forward bend, pay attention to the stretch of your back muscles and backs of legs; blood in head and arms. As you do your side stretch, pay attention to stretching in your chest, sides and neck.

Step 5: Assume a comfortable sitting posture, one you can hold for 15 to 20 minutes. This could be in a chair. Get comfortable and close your eyes when you are ready. Please note everything you are aware of: outside sounds, your bodily awareness, thoughts; note this awareness and do not change it. Then, notice shifting from outside sounds to thoughts of bodily awareness. After approximately five minutes of this, notice that breathing is occurring; again, not to change it but only to notice it. One can enhance this noticing by attaching the words ``breathing out" to the breath as it leaves the nostrils and ``breathing in" as the breath re-enters. As awareness shifts from breathing to thoughts of external sounds, allow that to happen and the return to ``breathing out-breathing in" (following the breath).

Continue this for five to seven minutes. At this point, try to incorporate some visual imagery in the form of a golden light with the in-breath. See yourself breathing in this golden light and watching it fill the inside of your body. This could be in a particle, vapor, smoke, or mist like form, whatever is comfortable for you. Visualize this light in your head, shoulders, chest and breath out any tensions in the form of a black color. Continue until you visually experience your whole body as being filled with this golden light. Experience that feeling. Stay with this experience for another minute or two. Then, become aware of your breath again, with your body sitting on the floor or chair (feeling grounded). When ready, open your eyes.

Step 6: Try this breathing exercise for 15 to 20 minutes daily until you are able to achieve full breathing and stress reduction in a progressively shorter period of time.

LAUGHTER

For many years I suffered from near constant attacks of depression. I eventually learned that I could achieve relief by engaging in physical exercise, even though the effect was temporary it was better than nothing.

One night, after a late workout (when I still worked out), sweaty and physically exhausted but mentally charged, I went home and – feeling my adrenalin high rapidly fading – pulled up YouTube on my computer. I scrolled through the offerings until I came upon some clips from the old Carol Burnett Show and settled on several that featured Tim Conway, a comedian that I consider to be better than most and as good as the very best. Tim Conway's humor was both visual and auditory and even the other actors cracked up over his antics.

I laughed so hard that my sides ached.

Next, I clicked on to some Robin Williams sketches and once again I was laughing so hard, at one point I looked down and was surprised to see that my ass was still there – I mean, I thought I had laughed it right off.

It's wonderful how, with the right motivator, you can take very serious things like politics, politicians, race disputes, religion, and war and make it humorous, just by adjusting your angle and focus, and asking different questions. Unless they abuse their bodies by over-indulging with drugs, food, or drink, you rarely hear about comedians dying young… and that's because laughter is so good for us. And it gets us thinking in wildly hilarious directions which results in feelings of joy and happiness.

It's good to be a human, huh?

Most things that feel good right out of the chute are deadly. Sugar? Tastes good. Very bad for you. Telling someone "what you really think of them" feels good at the time. But not always so good in the end. Haagen Dazs chocolate dark chocolate ice cream bars? Oooo, too good. But later...

Laughter, though? Just plain good for you.

That maybe explains those "less-than-handsome" guys of modest means who always have a hot chick on his arm. Apparently they make the girls laugh… always a better option than making them cry.

The moral is, if you want to live a long life, then draw every ounce of joy and pleasure from every moment, regardless of the situation. Except when tragedy strikes… that is a time for learning not for humor. If you start a comedy routine you're an idiot. But when you know how to move past the pain of loss quickly, regardless of what the loss is, you will survive and thrive in a harsh, demanding world.

That's what effective behavior modification should do… it should teach and condition your brain to be able to find the joy, the humor, or the possible benefit in any situation you could find yourself in

Learn how to squeeze happiness from the lemons in your life you will always overcome the sadness and/or devastation.

We show people how to make that happen through our Dynamic Discovery program. You have nothing to lose except a heart attack or a stroke... and everything to gain, maybe even a little loving.

So go ahead, laugh your butt off.

CONCLUSION

Now that you have read about our Stress program, please remember that recovery is a process, not necessarily a single event. Recovery is a way of living, a quality of feeling, and a mental attitude. Because you are reading this, you have likely started the recovery process, which probably began with the realization, or just a suspicion, that your life was not progressing in a way that was healthy.

The knowing or suspicion that something was amiss was likely what drew you to us – and that was enough for the recovery process to start. Recovery is a process that is often filled with moments of sharp, clear insights, and sometimes blazing realizations but, for the most part recovery is learning to live life from a new and different point of view. The challenge is to be open to learn new skills and to experiment with different points of view in new and creative ways.

Letting go of the pain and fear is a necessary part of the recovery process and as we let go, happiness, freedom and joy become a way of life, rather than just words spoken or read. I have seen that happen again and again. Joy and love of life is the reward for walking through the 'pain' of growth.

"Just as a map is not the territory but a guide to the territory, I hope that this book will prove to be a map to the territory of your relationships."

The amount of happiness that is available to you as you continue to apply your newfound skills and techniques is infinite because you define the goal at the top by the power of your increasing vision; the higher you climb the farther that you can see. And when you stop and rest and enjoy the view from your new vantage point, there is nothing sweeter.

There is no limit to the passion and meaning that you can derive from your journey.

You can incorporate any existing tool or program within the larger context of this journey as long as it makes you more powerful, awake and responsible. And that is your pathway to freedom.

Because your path is right there for you, I want you to remember that, no matter what happens, the path that you created is right before you all you have to do is walk the path, and you will feel the power of your design.

When I think of the wasted dreams, the unfulfilled lives and the lost opportunities in so many of the people around me I feel sad... sad and more committed than ever to disseminating Dynamic Discovery material through our website and the included blog postings (www.dynamicdiscovery.ca). But I don't see any of our programs as completed products; rather, I see Dynamic Discovery as something that can continue to evolve so as to enable us to work with people suffering from many of life's shattering problems.

Finally, let me now clarify some things about myself:

"I do not consider myself to be an 'expert' on anything – but I have lived to talk about the many traumatic events I have lived through. Some of those happenings involved loss of life." I believe that, like you, I am an intelligent person and I know that intelligent people can act stupid – where the term stupid means lacking intelligence or common sense – when convinced by an authority figure that they are stupid.

My knowledge and beliefs concerning human behavior came about over the course of many years as a result of working with people who sought my assistance to deal with a rather long list of personal problems. Some of those people have become friends.

Our programs are not about advice, they are about helping you find your way to a better life… as you determine it. By the way, if advice were all we need to build a better life, then all one would have to do is just stand on any street corner and, within time, you will be overwhelmed with advice. I believe this: advice by itself could provide the perfect answer but the reason why it is not enough is because the advice we receive seldom contains a detailed description of how to implement it.

Something to remember: The human being is the only creature on earth that is not a prisoner of its programming but the master of it. Therefore, none of us needs to live even a minute longer as we are, because we have been endowed with the ability to change ourselves.

Remember, we evaluate for wanted and unwanted not for right and wrong, or good and bad.

We show you how to self-evaluate for what is and what isn't.

You learn to measure yourself by your own yardstick.

I hope that this book has helped you or a loved one. If you need any further help feel free to reach out to me on my website. Two things I ask is: One share this book with someone that may need it. Two please scanning this code to leave a review. Thanks

ONLINE TESTS

http://www.psychologytoday.com/tests

http://psychologytoday.tests.psychtests.com/take_test.php ?idRegTest=1308

http://www.depression-anxiety-stress-test.org/take-the-test.html

http://www.nhs.uk/Conditions/stress-anxiety-depression/Pages/mood-self-assessment.aspx

http://www.15minutes4me.com/free-online-test-stress-anxiety-depression-burnout/

http://counsellingresource.com/lib/quizzes/depression-testing/goldberg-depression/

If you want to do more than observe and test, check out our Dynamic Discovery program at www.dynamicdiscovery.ca

This information is not intended to treat, diagnose, cure or prevent any disease. Please seek the guidance of a qualified health care provider before undertaking any recovery program.

SAMPLE OF FEAR

...HOW TO OVERCOME IT
...HOW TO TURN IT TO YOUR ADVANTAGE

BY GEORGE BISSETT

Introduction

While the intention of this book is to help you to identify and address your fears, its primary purpose is to turn your fears from a weakness to a strength.

Take a moment to let that concept sink in...
Turn your fears from a weakness to a strength.

Right now, you're probably thinking to yourself, "Is that actually possible?" And the simple answer from me is, "Yes, it is!"

Let's check out together some notable examples of 'overcoming' adversity and becoming 'accomplished'. Because of where I have lived for many years, the first example I choose is Saskatchewan, Canada's own Alvin Law.

Alvin Law

Alvin Law was born without arms. His birth mother, thinking it to be completely safe, took just a couple of those tiny Thalidomide pills. The effects were devastating and life changing for Alvin. Over 13,000 babies around the world were deformed in the early 1960s because Thalidomide, a morning sickness drug. Yet, what could so easily have become a tragic life-story did not turn out that way. Today, Alvin is a successful, independent and remarkable professional speaker. He is the proof that out of nothing can arise one of the most inspiring stories you will ever witness.

Since 1976, Alvin has played a direct role in raising over $150,000,000 for charity. He has also dabbled in acting, playing a role in a quirky creative film called Julien: Donkey Boy. He has also played an armless preacher in an episode of the hit television series, The X-Files. Alvin has appeared on countless telethons, media features and has been the subject of two award winning television documentaries. The first, 'Alvin, His Best Foot Forward', was shown across Canada in 1978. The second, 'Broken Promises', focused on the plight of Canada's Thalidomide victims and after its Canadian showing was seen on American Public Broadcastings 'Frontline'. Re-named 'Extraordinary People', it was nominated for an Emmy Award. Alvin has appeared on The Joan Rivers Show, "How'd They Do That" on CBS, CBC's 'What On Earth' and ABC's 'Frontrunners'. This segment about Alvin received an Emmy Award. Alvin often says, he always knew angels existed. In 1991, he met one and in 1993, he married Darlene and now lives with her and his son, Vance, in Calgary, Alberta.

Stephen Hawking

Stephen Hawking is easily one of the most brilliantly scientific minds on the planet. He has contributed groundbreaking work in the areas of physics and cosmology. He has also written a number of books, including the bestselling 'A Brief History of Time', which endeavors to explain some of the world's biggest mysteries.

Hawking has achieved all of this despite being diagnosed at the age of 21 with amyotrophic lateral sclerosis, also known as ALS or Lou Gehrig's disease. This is a disorder that includes weakness and muscle atrophy. Now 70 years old, Hawking is almost entirely paralyzed and must communicate using a device that can generate speech. He has three children, one of which has written three children's books with him.

Bethany Hamilton

At a very young age Hamilton began surfing. Disaster struck however and at the age of 13, an almost deadly shark attack resulted in the loss of her left arm. Incredibly she was back on her surfboard after just one month following the accident and only two years later, she scooped first place in the Explorer Women's Division of the NSSA National Championships. Now that's what we can call determination!

Oprah Winfrey

Billionaire Oprah Winfrey is best known for hosting her own internationally popular talk show from 1986 to 2011. She is also an actress, philanthropist, publisher and producer. Media giant Oprah Winfrey was born in the rural town of Kosciusko, Mississippi, on January 29th, 1954. In 1976, Winfrey moved to Baltimore, where she hosted a hit television chat show called, 'People Are Talking'. Following this, she was recruited by a Chicago TV station to host her own morning show. She later became the host of her own, wildly popular program, The Oprah Winfrey Show, which aired for 25 seasons, from 1986 to 2011. That same year, Winfrey launched her own TV network, the Oprah Winfrey Network.

Oprah Gail Winfrey had a troubled adolescence in a small farming community. She was sexually abused by a number of male relatives and friends of her mother, Vernita. Winfrey decided to move to Nashville to live with her father, Vernon, who was a barber and businessman. She entered Tennessee State University in 1971 and began working in radio and television broadcasting in Nashville.

Winfrey launched the Oprah Winfrey Show in 1986 as a nationally syndicated program. It was aired on 120 channels and had an audience of 10 million people. The show had grossed $125 million by the end of its first year, of which Winfrey received $30 million. She soon gained ownership of the program from ABC, drawing it under the control of her new production company, Harpo

Productions ('Oprah' spelled backwards) and making
more and more money from syndication.

Winfrey was born into poverty in rural Mississippi to a
teenage single mother and later raised in an inner-city
Milwaukee neighborhood. She experienced considerable
hardship during her childhood, saying she was raped at
age nine and became pregnant at 14. Her son died in
infancy. Sent to live with the man she calls her father, a
barber in Tennessee, Winfrey landed a job in radio while
still in high school and began co-anchoring the local
evening news at the age of 19. Her emotional ad-lib
delivery eventually got her transferred to the daytime-
talk-show arena and after boosting a third-rated local
Chicago talk show to first place, she launched her own
production company and became internationally
syndicated.

Howard Hughes
Howard Hughes was one of the wealthiest people in
history. He was worth $1.5 billion at the time of his death
back in 1976. During his life he achieved many things,
which included being a respected film director, producer,
aviation expert, philanthropist and businessman.

If you saw Leonardo DiCaprio's portrayal of Hughes in "The Aviator," you know that Hughes also suffered from extreme obsessive-compulsive disorder. As he got older, the condition worsened and he became a recluse. Due to serious chronic pain, as a result of multiple plane-related crashes, he became addicted to narcotic medicine. Despite the OCD and the chronic pain, Howard Hughes remains a legend throughout the world.

If you think that there wasn't a whole lot of fear experienced by those people, think again and imagine what it must have been like to know that without your permission and with no warning, you were born with, or developed what most people would see as a great 'handicap'.

There are several other men and women who prove the same point. I have included them at the end of the book.

If you like what you have read and are looking to read more by scanning this code back to Amazon.com

RESOURCES

Credit for much of my base of knowledge belongs to:

• The Alandel School and Clinic (hypnotherapy training).

• 20 years experience working as a counselor and employee assistance program manager for Human Resources Services Ltd. (HRS).

• The Heartview Foundation of Mandan, North Dakota, where I learned about addictions.

• 26 years of immersion in the program of Alcoholics Anonymous.

• 25 years of studying various programs/approaches such as NLP, Psychology, Cognitive Behavioural Therapy, Quantum Physics and Reality Therapy.

• Abraham Maslow's hierarchy of needs.

• Dr. William Glasser, a psychiatrist who developed Reality Therapy / Control Theory and is the father of

Reality Therapy and Control Theory and is also founder of the Reality Therapy Institute.

• The writings of Milton Erickson which drew upon his own experiences to provide examples of the power of the unconscious mind. He was largely self-taught.

• Dave Elman, who was self-taught and wrote "Hypnotherapy" which was self-published.

• The book Alcoholics Anonymous (commonly known as The Big Book), the members I've come to know and love both in AA and its sister organization, Alanon.

• The teachings of Socrates, especially those concerning inductive reasoning (to draw logical conclusions) and his Four basic Principles of Philosophy.

• The writings of Napoleon Hill, who enjoyed a long and successful career writing, teaching, lecturing about the principles of success, and whose work is still relevant for those seeking personal achievement and motivation.

• The writings of Carlos Castaneda – particularly The Teachings of Don Juan – who was an American author with a Ph. D in anthropology

• Tony Robbins - The Six Human Needs.

• Manfred Max-Neef (along with Antonio Elizalde and Martin Hopenhayn) developed the theory of Human Needs and Human-Scale Development.
Personal

Prior to developing the DYNAMIC DISCOVERY process I was presenting and leading a two day seminar program - I called "THE PERSONAL IMPROVEMENT SERIES" - that consisted of 4 topics, each of which were 4 hours in duration, typically presented on Saturday and Sunday. The 4 topics were: Intimate Relationships; Guilt; Co-Dependency, and; The Right To Choose and were sponsored by an Employee and Family Assistance Program (EFAP) provider who had contracts to provide psychological counseling services to various corporations and government agencies.

I worked with several groups of clients from whom I learned some things that were never on my agenda. I did not want to be a counselor or therapist, and I certainly did not want to be anyone's advisor; I just enjoyed presenting information to people who were interested in looking at ways to make changes in their lives. Those first clients lead me into this process of self-evaluation through their enthusiastic and active participation which turned my seminars (or workshops) into participatory group sessions.

The basis for my foundation book came about in December, 1995, while I was sorting my notes from 4 years of those group sessions because I wanted to create a document that could be used by some of my clients who wanted to understand the "hows" and "whys" of the process that unfolded during those group sessions. There is no way that I had the knowledge or training to – on my own – develop the DYNAMIC DISCOVERY process; it came from real life situations and the very real people who shared their thoughts and stories with the Group and who allowed me to learn from them and keep some notes on what was happening during those early sessions because the process works through the group members and not through the group leader. The notes have never been used for reports to employers or others persons outside the Group and for reasons of respect and confidentiality real client names have not been used. Because this is a self-evaluation process there are no experts or gurus; all I know that my clients don't know is the progression of the process and what the next question will be. I am not an expert or a guru - just someone privileged to share information that other non-experts have provided to me, in a format that a broad range of people can easily grasp and understand.

ABOUT THE AUTHOR

George has lived and/or worked in all ten Canadian provinces and three territories, as well as having lived and/or worked in 28 of the 50 United States.

He had a problem with alcohol but for more than 26 years (since September 9, 1988) he has not used intoxicants of any kind. Achieving sobriety led to his interest in human behavior and, in particular, why we humans do what we do. His interest and work in the field of human behavior eventually lead me to working for an Employee Assistance Program as both a counselor and manager as well as leading and facilitating workshops and seminars. Prior to developing the DYNAMIC DISCOVERY process he was presenting and leading a two day seminar program titled "THE PERSONAL IMPROVEMENT SERIES" that consisted of 4 topics: Intimate Relationships; Guilt; Co-Dependency, and; The Right To Choose. The back and forth interactions with those seminar clients was enthusiastic and instructive, which led him into using a process of self-evaluation and eventually turned his seminars and workshops into participatory group sessions focused on unwanted and wanted behaviors and how to move from the former to the latter.

He first became interested in the self-evaluation process when he read some of the works of American philosopher and psychologist William James (1890, 1892) who developed a basic approach to self-evaluations when he studied and wrote about his theories on Mind cure and the principles of psychology which set the stage for multidimensional and hierarchical models of the self. The formal format for the Dynamic Discovery program came about in December, 1995, while he was sorting his notes from 4 years of those two day seminar sessions because he wanted to create a document that could be used by some of his clients who wanted to understand the "hows" and "whys" of the process that had unfolded during those group sessions... from real life situations and the very real people who shared their thoughts and stories with the Group and who allowed him to learn from them and keep some notes on what was happening during those early sessions.

Career Path

His first career choice was the Royal Canadian Air Force and he lucked into being part of a Para-Rescue unit. Being a Jumper appealed to his sense of adventure and pumped up his esteem because Jumpers were few and far between. However, he will admit to having feelings of superiority because the greatest danger to most Airmen and Airwomen was the possibility of a life-endangering paper cut.

He spent the next 25 years as a builder and real estate developer as well as consulting on approximately 3 million square feet of commercial buildings; mostly hotels and casinos.

Professional Development

Certified Hypnotherapist

Certified Lifeskills Trainer and Coach

Certified Building Technologist

Certificate in Alternative Dispute Resolution

Professional Member, International Facility Management
Association

Council of Canadian Administrative Tribunals
(Administrative Law)

International Association of Industrial Accident Boards
and Commissions (Adjudicative Law)

Sales and Marketing Council, Canadian Home Builders
Association

dynamic discovery
a process of self-evaluation

"Dynamic Discovery is a personal development process that will lead you to an understanding of how to take control of your life ... again."

Our positive and relaxed atmosphere enables our members to use the group process to make effective and meaningful changes in their individual lives. We combine a supportive, non-critical group environment with an innovative process for personal change.

Discover how to get started on getting what you really want from life. Discover how to move from unwanted behaviours to wanted behaviours.

Discover how to regain control of your life and how to achieve balance in all aspects (mental /physical / spiritual).

Discover how to improve your personal image. Discover how to make gain without pain.

Discover how to deal with personal issues, such as :

Marital/relationship problems.
Pre-marital counsel.
Moving past a "stuck – point".
Weight / fitness management.
Relapse prevention (addictions).
Declining work performance.
Corporate downsizing ("outplacement").
Early retirement.
Sexual / physical abuse.
And any other thinking, feeling, or doing problems humans can have.
Dynamic Discovery is a process of self-evaluation, based upon getting what you want and dealing with your needs.

All you need to bring with you is an open-mind.

DISCLAIMER

www.ingramcontent.com/pod-product-compliance
Lightning Source LLC
Chambersburg PA
CBHW060507030426
42337CB00015B/1774